The Beginner's Guide to a Plant-based Diet

Easy Beginners Cookbook with Plant-Based Recipes for Healthy Eating & a 3-Week Plant-Based Diet Meal Plan to Reset & Energize Your Body

monetary loss due to the information herein, either directly or indirectly.

Respective authors own all copyrights not held by the publisher.

The information herein is offered for informational purposes solely and is universal as so. The presentation of the information is without a contract or any type of guarantee assurance.

The trademarks that are used are without any consent, and the publication of the trademark is without permission or backing by the trademark owner. All trademarks and brands within this book are for clarifying purposes only and are owned by the owners themselves, not affiliated with this document.

Table of Contents

INTRODUCTION

Choosing the perfect diet plan can be confusing thanks to the variety of diet plans available these days. Irrespective of what diet plan you opt for, almost all nutritionists and dietitians across the globe recommend diet plans that limit processed foods and that are based more on whole and fresh foods. The Plant-Based Diet is based on these universally preferred foods.

The primary focus of a plant-based, whole-food diet plan is to minimize the intake of processed foods as much as possible and consume more plant-based, whole natural foods that are proven to be beneficial for not only improving your health but also stimulating effective weight loss. This introduction is going to clear away all ambiguities and doubts regarding the whole-food, plant-based diet plan and provide logical explanations to the benefits it offers.

What is a Whole-Food, Plant-Based (WFPB) Diet Plan?

There are no hard and fast rules and regulations to configure a whole-food plant-based (WFPB) diet plan. The reason for this is that it is not just a diet plan but a complete lifestyle change. Usually, plant-based diet plans are critically dependent to the extent where you cut off animal-based foods from your diet completely. To avoid any confusion, here are a few factors that are a must for a whole-food plant-based diet plan:

1. Limit animal-based foods
2. Focus more on natural, whole or minimally processed foods
3. Eat plants like legumes, seeds, veggies, fruits, whole grains, and nuts to your diet plan abundantly
4. Eliminate refined foods including processed oils, white flour, and added sugars
5. Favor organic and locally-sourced food when possible

Most of the above traits are also found in vegetarian and vegan diet plans, which is why the whole-food plant-based diet is easily confused with them. But, trust us, they are different. A vegan diet eliminates all animal-related foods, including seafood, dairy, honey, meat, and poultry. On the other hand, vegetarian diets exclude meat and poultry but typically allow seafood, dairy products, eggs, and honey.

Contrary to them, the whole-food plant-based diet plan is more flexible and forgiving. The food is mostly plant-based, but you can also eat animal-based products in moderation. The extent of animal-related foods in your diet plan depends on your personal choice of entirely not eating them or consuming them in small amounts. In short, a whole-food plant-based diet plan is comprised of plant-based foods with a minimal amount of animal-related products and processed foods.

The Benefits of a Whole-Food Plant-Based Diet (WFPB) Plan

There are numerous benefits of switching to the whole-food plant-based diet plan ranging from improved health to being eco-friendlier. Consider the benefits if you're unsure about making the switch.

1. Weight Loss and Overall Improved Health

Obesity is considered to be an epidemic nowadays. Shockingly, more than 69 percent of adults in the United States are considered obese or overweight. Making changes in your diet and your whole lifestyle can lead to drastic weight loss when done properly. The impacts of these changes can be promising and long lasting. There are numerous studies that determined plant-based diet plans are very effective for weight loss.

The whole-food plant-based diet plan is rich in fiber and restricts processed foods while forbidding soda, refined grains, fast food, candy, and added sugars, making it ideal for weight loss. An overall assessment of 12 research studies found that people who followed plant-based diet plans lost more weight (2 kg, in almost 18 weeks as compared to non-plant-based diet followers). A plant-based diet plan can also keep you from gaining weight over a longer period.

2. Beneficial in Various Health Issues

Besides aiding in weight loss, a whole-food plant-based diet has also been proven to help lower the risks of various chronic health conditions.

- Cardiac Conditions

This is the most widely-known benefit of whole-food plant-based diets as they have higher probabilities of keeping your cardiac health sound. But, the strength of this benefit is dependent on the types and quality of the food in your diet plan. Major research done on over 200,000 people concluded that the risk of having heart disease was lower in those people whose diet plan was plant-based and was rich in whole grains, veggies, nuts, legumes, and fruits than those who were following non-plant based diets.

But, plant-based diet plans that are unhealthy because of the inclusion of fruit juices, refined grains, and sugary drinks showed an increased risk of cardiac complications. This is why, it is very important to stick to the right foods and follow a healthy plant-based diet plan.

- Cancer

According to various research studies, a plant-based diet plan can lower risks of various forms of cancer. A study of over 69,000 people found that the risk of gastrointestinal cancer was very low for vegetarian diet followers, especially for Lacto-ovo vegetarian diet followers (the ones who consume both dairy and eggs).

In another study of over 77,000 people, it was proven that there was a 22 percent reduced risk of having colorectal cancer in those who followed a vegetarian diet plan than those who didn't. The safest was pescatarians (those vegetarians who consume fish) as they had a significant 43 percent lower risk of colorectal cancer than non-vegetarian diet plan followers.

- Cognitive Decline

There are various studies that found that diet plans high in fruit and veggie content can prevent or slow Alzheimer's disease and cognitive decline in adults. The reason is that many foods in plant-based diet plans are high in antioxidants and plant compounds that act as protective agents against the development of Alzheimer's disease and reversing cognitive damage.

A review of nine research studies of around 31,000 people found that those who consumed more veggies and fruits had a significant 20 percent lower risk of having dementia or cognitive impairment.

- Diabetes

A whole-food plant-based diet plan can play a significant role in lowering the risk of contracting diabetes or managing the illness. In a study involving over 200,000 people, it was proven that there was a 34 percent reduced risk of having diabetes if you followed a healthy, plant-based diet in comparison to an unhealthy, non-plant based plan.

In another research study, it was proven that both Lacto-ovo vegetarian and vegan diet plans could lower the risk of type 2 diabetes by a whopping 50 percent in comparison to non-plant-based diet plans. Plant-based diet plans are also known to cause improvements in blood sugar level control in people with diabetes as compared to non-plant based diets.

3. More Eco-friendly Diet

The whole-food plant-based diet plan is not only beneficial in terms of health but also proven to be better for the ecosystem. Plant-based diet plan followers tend to have a smaller effect on the environment in comparison to other diet plan followers.

Sustainable eating approaches can help lower greenhouse gas effects as well as land and water consumption required for factory farming. These factors are known to be the major cause of harm to the ecosystem and overall global warming.

Around 64 different research studies found that diets with a minimal amount of animal-based foods like pescatarian, vegetarian, and vegan diet plans are known to be the most beneficial in terms of the environment. These studies also found that the transition of Western diet plans to a healthy, plant-based diet plan can result in 50 percent lower water usage and a significant 70 percent reduction in land usage and greenhouse gas emissions.

In addition to this, lowering animal-based food and choosing sustainable and locally-grown products can boost the economy and lower dependency on unsustainable practices like factory farming.

Foods Allowed on a Whole-Food Plant-Based Diet (WFPB) Plan

Most people focus on animal-based products as a primary food source ranging from bacon and eggs for breakfast to steak for dinner. The plant-based diet plan focuses on plant-based foods as the primary food source for most of the meals. If you have an urge to eat animal-based foods, go for a significantly smaller quantity and a higher-quality product. Animal-based foods like meat, seafood, eggs, dairy, and poultry should be used as a side dish or a compliment to the primary plant-based meal, instead of being the main part of the dish. The following list will make the food choices easier for you while following the whole-food plant-based diet plan

➢ **Veggies:** spinach, broccoli, asparagus, kale, tomatoes, carrots, peppers, cauliflower, etc.

➢ **Fruits:** pears, bananas, berries, pineapples, citrus fruits, peaches, etc.

- ➢ **Whole grains:** barley, rolled oats, quinoa, brown rice, brown rice pasta, farro, etc.
- ➢ **Healthy fats:** coconut oil, avocados, unsweetened coconut, olive oil, etc.
- ➢ **Starchy veggies:** butternut squash, potatoes, sweet potatoes, etc.
- ➢ **Legumes:** peanuts, peas, black beans, lentils, chickpeas, etc.
- ➢ **Nuts, nut butter, and seeds:** tahini, sunflower seeds, cashews, macadamia nuts, almonds, natural peanut butter (sugar-free), pumpkin seeds, etc.
- ➢ **Plant-based milk (unsweetened):** cashew milk, almond milk, coconut milk, etc.
- ➢ **Seasonings, herbs, and spices:** salt, turmeric, basil, black pepper, rosemary, curry, etc.
- ➢ **Condiments:** soy sauce, lemon juice, salsa, vinegar, nutritional yeast, mustard, etc.
- ➢ **Plant-based protein:** tempeh, tofu, and plant-based protein powders or sources without artificial ingredients or added sugars in them.
- ➢ **Drinks:** sparkling water, tea, coffee, etc.

In case you want to truly supplement your plant-based diet plan with some animal-based products, choose high-quality products from any grocery store, or preferably grab them from local farms for better quality. These include the following products:

> **Eggs:** choose pasture-raised if possible.

> **Poultry:** go for free-range and organic if possible.

> **Pork & beef:** choose grass-fed or pasture-raised if possible.

> **Seafood:** opt for wild caught from sustainable fisheries if possible.

> **Dairy products:** grab organic dairy products from animals that are pasture raised if possible.

Foods to Avoid or Limit on the Whole-Food Plant-Based Diet (WFPB) Plan

The entire whole-food plant-based diet plan is based on adding natural food to your plate and avoiding as much artificially-produced food as possible. There is no space for heavily processed foods on a plant-based diet plan. This means that while you are purchasing grocery items, choose fresh foods. When you do buy packaged food, opt for the ones with the least amount of ingredients.

Avoid the following:

> **Fast food:** cheeseburgers, chicken nuggets, French fries, hot dogs, etc.

> **Added sugars and sweets:** sugary cereals, soda, pastries, table sugar, sweet tea, juice, candy, cookies, etc.

- ➢ **Refined grains:** bagels, white pasta, white rice, white bread, etc.
- ➢ **Artificial sweeteners:** Splenda, Equal, Sweet'N Low, etc.
- ➢ **Processed animal products:** beef jerky, bacon, sausage, lunch meats, etc.
- ➢ **Processed vegan-friendly foods:** plant-based meats like Tofurkey, vegan butter, faux cheeses, etc.

Even if you include healthy animal-based products in your whole-food plant-based diet plan, you will have to limit the following foods for a proper WFPB diet plan.

Limit the following:

- ➢ Pork
- ➢ Game Meats
- ➢ Sheep
- ➢ Beef
- ➢ Eggs
- ➢ Dairy
- ➢ Poultry
- ➢ Seafood

CHAPTER 1 «THE PLANT-BASED 21-DAY MEAL PLAN»

Week 1 Meal Plan

Day 1
Breakfast: Creamy Chocolate Shake
Lunch: Sniffle Soup
Dinner: Rustic Pasta

Day 2
Breakfast: Hidden Kale Smoothie
Lunch: French Lentil Soup with Paprika
Dinner: Vegan Lasagna

Day 3
Breakfast: Blueberry Protein Shake
Lunch: Squash Soup
Dinner: Garlic Alfredo Pasta

Day 4
Breakfast: Raspberry Lime Smoothie
Lunch: Chickpea Lentil Soup
Dinner: Golden Pasta

Day 5

Breakfast: Peppermint Monster Smoothie

Lunch: Beans and Lentils Soup

Dinner: Creamy Spinach Pasta

Day 6

Breakfast: Almond Banana Granola

Lunch: Quinoa Salad

Dinner: Haka Noodles

Day 7

Breakfast: Eggless Omelet

Lunch: Devilish Ramen

Dinner: Veggie Stir Fry

Week 2 Meal Plan

Day 1
Breakfast: Polenta
Lunch: Basil Noodle Salad
Dinner: French Potato Salad

Day 2
Breakfast: Lemon Apple Breakfast
Lunch: Kale Salad
Dinner: Grilled Mushrooms

Day 3
Breakfast: Oats and Chia Bowl
Lunch: Penne Pasta Salad
Dinner: Sweet Potato Noodles

Day 4
Breakfast: Grilled Tofu
Lunch: Tofu Noodle Bowl
Dinner: Brown Rice Stir Fry

Day 5
Breakfast: Grilled Pineapple
Lunch: Teriyaki Stir Fry
Dinner: Sweet Potato Hash

Day 6
Breakfast: Hot Grilled Watermelon
Lunch: Garlic Alfredo Pasta
Dinner: Roasted Chickpeas

Day 7
Breakfast: Creamy Chocolate Shake
Lunch: Baked Sesame Fries
Dinner: Niçoise Salad

Week 3 Meal Plan

Day 1
Breakfast: Winter Refresher
Lunch: Tempeh Bacon Hash
Dinner: Baked Sesame Fries

Day 2
Breakfast: Veggie Breakfast Hash
Lunch: French Lentil Soup with Paprika
Dinner: Vegan Lasagna

Day 3
Breakfast: Pumpkin Smoothie
Lunch: French Potato Salad
Dinner: Garlic Alfredo Pasta

Day 4
Breakfast: Chocolate Avocado Mousse
Lunch: Quinoa Salad
Dinner: Haka Noodles

Day 5
Breakfast: Berry Lime Smoothie
Lunch: Quinoa Salad
Dinner: Teriyaki Stir Fry

Day 6

Breakfast: Banana Green Smoothie

Lunch: Basil Noodle Salad

Dinner Grilled Mushrooms

Day 7

Breakfast: Tempeh Bacon Hash

Lunch: Chickpea Lentil Soup

Dinner: Creamy Spinach Pasta

CHAPTER 2 «SMOOTHIES & BREAKFAST»

Creamy Chocolate Shake

Ingredients:

- 2 frozen ripe bananas, chopped
- 1/3 cup frozen strawberries
- 2 tbsp cocoa powder
- 2 tbsp salted almond butter
- 2 cups unsweetened vanilla almond milk
- 1 dash Stevia or agave nectar
- 1/3 cup ice

How to prepare:

1. Add all ingredients in a blender and blend until smooth.
2. Take out and serve.

Preparation time: 10 minutes

Cooking time: 0 minutes

Total time: 10 minutes

Servings: 2

Nutritional Values:

- *Calories 312*
- *Total Fat 14 g*
- *Saturated Fat 1 g*
- *Cholesterol 0 mg*
- *Sodium 0 mg*
- *Total Carbs 48 g*
- *Fiber 7.5 g*
- *Sugar 27 g*
- *Protein 6.2 g*
- *Potassium 311 mg*

Hidden Kale Smoothie

Ingredients:

- 1 medium ripe banana, peeled and sliced
- ½ cup frozen mixed berries
- 1 tbsp hulled hemp seeds
- 2 cups frozen or fresh kale
- 2/3 cup 100% pomegranate juice
- 2¼ cups filtered water

How to prepare:
1. Add all ingredients in a blender and blend until smooth.
2. Take out and serve.

Preparation time: 5 minutes

Cooking time: 0 minutes

Total time: 5 minutes

Servings: 2

Nutritional Values:

- *Calories 178*
- *Total Fat 1.8 g*
- *Saturated Fat 0.3 g*
- *Cholesterol 0 mg*
- *Sodium 33 mg*
- *Total Carbs 37.8 g*
- *Fiber 4.3 g*
- *Sugar 20.4 g*
- *Protein 4.1 g*
- *Potassium 785 mg*

Blueberry Protein Shake

Ingredients:

- ½ cup cottage cheese or low-fat yogurt
- 3 tbsp vanilla protein powder
- ½ cup frozen blueberries
- ½ tsp maple extract
- ¼ tsp vanilla extract
- 2 tsp flaxseed meal
- Sweetener of choice (to taste)
- 10-15 ice cubes
- ¼ cup water

How to prepare:

1. Add all ingredients in a blender and blend until smooth.
2. Take out and serve.

Preparation time: 5 minutes

Cooking time: 0 minutes

Total time: 5 minutes

Servings: 1

Nutritional Values:

*   *Calories 230*
*   *Total Fat 5 g*
*   *Saturated Fat 1.9 g*
*   *Cholesterol 0 mg*
*   *Sodium 0 mg*
*   *Total Carbs 18 g*
*   *Fiber 3.1 g*
*   *Sugar 9 g*
*   *Protein 27.5 g*
*   *Potassium 210 mg*

Raspberry Lime Smoothie

Ingredients:

- 1 cup water
- 1 cup frozen or fresh raspberries
- 1 large frozen banana (peel and freeze before making)
- 2 tbsp fresh lime juice
- 1 tsp coconut oil
- 1 tsp agave

How to prepare:

1. Add all ingredients in a blender and blend until smooth.
2. Take out and serve

Preparation time: 5 minutes

Cooking time: 0 minutes

Total time: 5 minutes

Servings: 2

Nutritional Values:

- *Calories 123*
- *Total Fat 2.9 g*
- *Saturated Fat 2.1 g*
- *Cholesterol 0 mg*
- *Sodium 5 mg*
- *Total Carbs 26.1 g*
- *Fiber 6 g*
- *Sugar 13.4 g*
- *Protein 1.5 g*
- *Potassium 350 mg*

Peppermint Monster Smoothie

Ingredients:

- 1 large frozen banana, peeled
- 1½ cups non-dairy milk
- A handful of fresh mint leaves, stems removed
- 1-2 handfuls spinach

How to prepare:

1. Add all ingredients in a blender and blend until smooth.
2. Take out and serve

Preparation time: 5 minutes
Cooking time: 0 minutes

Total time: 5 minutes

Servings: 1

Nutritional Values:

- *Calories 451*
- *Total Fat 18.6 g*
- *Saturated Fat 10.2 g*
- *Cholesterol 40 mg*
- *Sodium 271 mg*
- *Total Carbs 54.8 g*
- *Fiber 4.8 g*
- *Sugar 38.7 g*
- *Protein 18.4 g*
- *Potassium 1,511 mg*

Almond Banana Granola

Ingredients:

- 8 cups rolled oats
- 2 cups dates, pitted and chopped
- 2 ripe bananas, peeled and chopped
- 1 tsp almond extract
- 1 tsp salt

How to prepare:

1. Preheat oven to 275 degrees F.
2. Add oats to a bowl.
3. Take a baking sheet and line it with parchment paper.
4. Take a saucepan and add 1 cup water to it.
5. Place dates in the saucepan and heat them for 10 minutes.

6. Remove from heat.
7. Add heated mixture, bananas, almond extract, and salt to a blender.
8. Blend until smooth.
9. Add this mixture to the bowl with the oats and mix well.
10. Transfer the mixture to the lined baking sheets and spread it out evenly.
11. Bake for 40 to 50 minutes until crispy, stirring after 10 minutes.
12. Let cool and serve.

Preparation time: 15 minutes
Cooking time: 50 minutes
Total time: 65 minutes
Servings: 8

Nutritional Values:
- *Calories 463*
- *Total Fat 5.6 g*
- *Saturated Fat 1 g*
- *Cholesterol 0 mg*
- *Sodium 297 mg*
- *Total Carbs 95.6 g*
- *Fiber 12.6 g*
- *Sugar 32.7 g*
- *Protein 12.2 g*
- *Potassium 695 mg*

Eggless Omelet

Ingredients:

- 1 cup chickpea flour
- ½ tsp onion powder
- ½ tsp garlic powder
- ¼ tsp white pepper
- ¼ tsp black pepper
- 1/3 cup nutritional yeast
- ½ tsp baking soda
- 3 green onions (white and green parts), chopped

How to prepare:

1. Add all ingredients to a bowl and mix well.
2. Heat a frying pan on medium heat.

3. Pour batter into the frying pan.
4. As it cooks, flip the omelet.
5. When the underside is cooked, flip it again and cook for 1 minute.
6. Serve and enjoy.

Preparation time: 10 minutes
Cooking time: 15 minutes
Total time: 25 minutes
Servings: 3

Nutritional Values:

- *Calories 314*
- *Total Fat 5.1 g*
- *Saturated Fat 0.6 g*
- *Cholesterol 0 mg*
- *Sodium 240 mg*
- *Total Carbs 50.5 g*
- *Fiber 16.6 g*
- *Sugar 7.7 g*
- *Protein 21.5 g*
- *Potassium 1,063 mg*

Polenta

Ingredients:

- ¼ cup brown rice syrup
- 2 pears, peeled, cored, and diced
- 1 cup fresh or dried cranberries
- 1 tsp ground cinnamon
- 1 cup Basic Polenta, kept warm

How to prepare:

1. Take a saucepan and heat the brown rice syrup.
2. Add in the pears, polenta, cranberries, and cinnamon and cook for 10 minutes, stirring occasionally.
3. Serve and enjoy.

Preparation time: 5 minutes

Cooking time: 10 minutes

Total time: 15 minutes

Servings: 4

Nutritional Values:

- *Calories 178*
- *Total Fat 0.3 g*
- *Saturated Fat 0 g*
- *Cholesterol 0 mg*
- *Sodium 17 mg*
- *Total Carbs 44.4 g*
- *Fiber 4.9 g*
- *Sugar 23.9 g*
- *Protein 1.9 g*
- *Potassium 170 mg*

Lemon Apple Breakfast

Ingredients:

- 4 to 5 medium apples (any variety), cut into large pieces
- 5 to 6 dates, pitted
- Juice of 1 lemon (about 3 tbsp)
- 2 tbsp walnuts (about 6 walnut halves)
- ¼ tsp ground cinnamon

How to prepare:

1. In a food processor, add dates, lemon juice, walnuts, cinnamon, and 3 quarters of the apple in it.
2. Grind together until a crumbly mixture forms.
3. Add in the remaining apples and pulse it until crumbled.
4. Serve and enjoy.

Preparation time: 15 minutes

Cooking time: 0 minutes

Total time: 15 minutes

Servings: 2

Nutritional Values:

- *Calories 409*
- *Total Fat 5.7 g*
- *Saturated Fat 0.3 g*
- *Cholesterol 0 mg*
- *Sodium 6 mg*
- *Total Carbs 96.7 g*
- *Fiber 16.2 g*
- *Sugar 73.9 g*
- *Protein 4 g*
- *Potassium 802 mg*

Oats and Chia Bowl

Ingredients:

- ¾ cup gluten-free rolled oats
- ¼ cup plant milk
- ½ cup water
- 1 heaping tbsp chia seeds
- 1 tbsp maple syrup
- ¼ tsp cinnamon

How to prepare:

1. Place all ingredients in a jar and mix well.
2. Store in the refrigerator.

3. Serve with any fruit you like and enjoy.

Preparation time: 10 minutes

Cooking time: 0 minutes

Total time: 10 minutes

Servings: 1

Nutritional Values:

- *Calories 127*
- *Total Fat 5.4 g*
- *Saturated Fat 0.4 g*
- *Cholesterol 0 mg*
- *Sodium 6 mg*
- *Total Carbs 22.6 g*
- *Fiber 5.7 g*
- *Sugar 11.9 g*
- *Protein 3.6 g*
- *Potassium 144 mg*

CHAPTER 3 «SOUPS & SALAD RECIPES»

Sniffle Soup

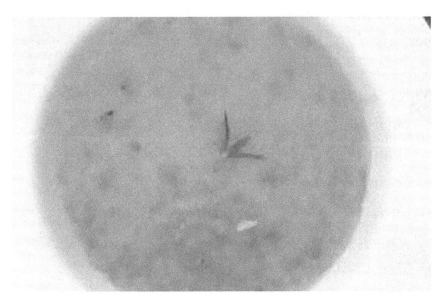

Ingredients:
- 1½ tbsp plus 4 cups water, divided
- 1½ cups onion, diced
- 1 cup carrot, diced
- 1 cup celery, diced
- 3 large cloves garlic, minced
- 1 tsp paprika
- 1 tsp mild curry powder
- ½ tsp sea salt
- ¼ tsp dried thyme

- Freshly ground black pepper, to taste
- 2 cups dried red lentils
- 3 cups vegetable stock
- 1½ tbsp apple cider vinegar

How to prepare:
1. Heat a large pot over medium heat.
2. Add all ingredients to the pot and stir occasionally.
3. Cook for 8 minutes.
4. Increase heat and bring it to a boil.
5. Once it is boiled, let it simmer for 25 minutes.
6. Serve and enjoy.

Preparation time: 10 minutes
Cooking time: 33 minutes
Total time: 43 minutes
Servings: 6

Nutritional Values:
- *Calories 290*
- *Total Fat 0.9 g*
- *Saturated Fat 0.1 g*
- *Cholesterol 0 mg*
- *Sodium 200 mg*
- *Total Carbs 52.7 g*
- *Fiber 22.9 g*
- *Sugar 7.1 g*
- *Protein 18.3 g*
- *Potassium 912 mg*

French Lentil Soup with Paprika

Ingredients:

- Splash water
- 1½ cups onion, diced
- 1 cup carrot, cut into disks
- 4- 5 cloves garlic, minced
- 1½ tsp dried thyme
- 1¼ to 1½ tsp smoked paprika
- 1 tsp Dijon mustard
- ¾ tsp sea salt
- Freshly ground black pepper, to taste
- 2 cups French lentils, rinsed
- 2 cups vegan vegetable stock
- 5 cups water
- ¼ cup tomato paste

- 1 bay leaf

How to prepare:
1. Heat a large pot over medium heat.
2. Add all ingredients in it to the pot and cook for 8 minutes, stirring occasionally.
3. Increase heat and bring it to a boil.
4. Once it is boiled, let it simmer for 35 minutes.
5. Remove bay leaf.
6. Serve and enjoy.

Preparation time: 10 minutes
Cooking time: 43 minutes
Total time: 53 minutes
Servings: 5

Nutritional Values:
- *Calories 109*
- *Total Fat 0.9 g*
- *Saturated Fat 0.5 g*
- *Cholesterol 0 mg*
- *Sodium 200 mg*
- *Total Carbs 26.1 g*
- *Fiber 8.3 g*
- *Sugar 8.6 g*
- *Protein 5.7 g*
- *Potassium 431 mg*

Squash Soup

Ingredients:

- 3 lb butternut squash or other deep orange winter squash, whole and unpeeled
- 1 large or 2 small onions, whole and unpeeled
- 2 cups water plus more (if desired) to thin
- ½ cup raw cashews, presoaked and drained
- 1 tbsp lemon juice, freshly squeezed
- 1 tsp fresh rosemary
- 1 tsp sea salt
- ¼ tsp cinnamon
- 1/8 tsp allspice
- 1 medium-large clove garlic, minced

How to prepare:
1. Preheat oven to 450 F.
2. Take a baking dish and line it with parchment paper.
3. Place onion and squash on the baking dish and bake for an hour.
4. Take a blender and add water, cashews, lemon juice, rosemary, sea salt, cinnamon, allspice, and garlic.
5. Puree until smooth.
6. Chop baked onions and squash and transfer to the blender with the skin and seeds removed.
7. Blend until smooth.
8. Transfer the soup to a pot and heat over low heat for 3 to 5 minutes and serve.

Preparation time: 10 minutes
Cooking time: 1 hour 5 minutes
Total time: 1 hour 15 minutes
Servings: 4

Nutritional Values:
- *Calories 125*
- *Total Fat 8.2 g*
- *Saturated Fat 1.6 g*
- *Cholesterol 0 mg*
- *Sodium 478 mg*
- *Total Carbs 11.4 g*
- *Fiber 2.1 g*
- *Sugar 3.4 g*
- *Protein 3.7 g*
- *Potassium 292 mg*

Chickpea Lentil Soup

Ingredients:

- Water
- 2 cups onion, diced
- ¾ tsp sea salt
- Freshly ground black pepper, to taste
- 1 tsp mustard seeds
- 1 tsp cumin seeds
- 1½ tsp paprika
- ½ tsp dried oregano
- ½ tsp dried thyme
- 1 cup dried red lentils
- 3½ cups chickpeas, cooked
- 2 cups tomatoes, chopped
- 3 cups vegetable stock

- 2 cups water
- 2 dried bay leaves
- ¼ cup fresh lemon juice

How to prepare:
1. Heat a large pot over medium heat.
2. Add all ingredients to it and cook for 6 minutes, stirring occasionally.
3. Increase heat and bring it to a boil.
4. Once it is boiled, let it simmer for 25 minutes.
5. Remove bay leaf.
6. Serve and enjoy.

Preparation time: 10 minutes
Cooking time: 31 minutes
Total time: 41 minutes
Servings: 6

Nutritional Values:
- *Calories 578*
- *Total Fat 9 g*
- *Saturated Fat 1.9 g*
- *Cholesterol 0 mg*
- *Sodium 634 mg*
- *Total Carbs 98 g*
- *Fiber 32.1 g*
- *Sugar 17.7 g*
- *Protein 32.1 g*
- *Potassium 1565 mg*

Beans and Lentils Soup

Ingredients:

- 2 tbsp water
- 1½ cups onion, diced
- 3 cups potatoes, cut in chunks
- ½ cup celery, diced
- 1 cup carrots, diced
- 4-5 cloves garlic, minced
- 1½ tsp dried rosemary leaves
- 1 tsp dried thyme leaves
- 1½ tsp ground mustard
- 1 tsp sea salt
- Freshly ground black pepper, to taste
- 1 cup green lentils, rinsed
- 2 cups vegetable stock
- 5 cups water

- 1 tbsp red miso
- 1½ tbsp blackstrap molasses
- 2 dried bay leaves
- 15-oz can white beans

How to prepare:
1. Heat a large pot over medium heat.
2. Add all ingredients to it and cook for 8 minutes, stirring occasionally.
3. Increase heat and bring it to a boil.
4. Once it is boiled, let it cook for 40 minutes.
5. Remove bay leaf.
6. Serve and enjoy.

Preparation time: 10 minutes
Cooking time: 48 minutes
Total time: 58 minutes
Servings: 4

Nutritional Values:
- *Calories 292*
- *Total Fat 2.3 g*
- *Saturated Fat 1.2 g*
- *Cholesterol 0 mg*
- *Sodium 1070 mg*
- *Total Carbs 61.7 g*
- *Fiber 11.3 g*
- *Sugar 10.5 g*
- *Protein 13.7 g*
- *Potassium 1,272 mg*

Quinoa Salad

Ingredients:

Quinoa:
- 1 cup quinoa
- 1 pinch sea salt
- 1 tsp curry powder
- 2 cups water

Dressing:
- 4 tbsp green curry paste
- 3 tbsp tahini
- 2 tbsp lemon juice
- 1 tbsp maple syrup
- 1 pinch each salt
- 1 pinch black pepper

- Water (to thin)

How to prepare:
1. Add quinoa to a saucepan and cook for 2 minutes stirring occasionally.
2. Add in water, salt, and curry powder and bring to boil.
3. Once boiling, reduce heat to simmer for 20 minutes until all water absorbs then allow to slightly cool.
4. Meanwhile, prepare the dressing by whisking together curry, tahini, lemon juice, maple syrup, salt, and pepper.
5. Add this mixture to cooled quinoa and mix well.
6. Serve and enjoy.

Preparation time: 30 minutes
Cooking time: 20 minutes
Total time: 50 minutes
Servings: 4

Nutritional Values:
- *Calories 333*
- *Total Fat 15.1 g*
- *Saturated Fat 1.7 g*
- *Cholesterol 0 mg*
- *Sodium 522 mg*
- *Total Carbs 43 g*
- *Fiber 5.3 g*
- *Sugar 5 g*
- *Protein 9 g*
- *Potassium 320 mg*

French Potato Salad

Ingredients:

Potatoes + vegetables:
- 2 lb baby yellow potatoes, rinsed and sliced
- 1 pinch sea salt and black pepper
- 1 tbsp apple cider vinegar
- 1 cup green onion, diced

Dressing:
- 2½ tbsp spicy brown mustard (or Dijon mustard)
- 3 cloves garlic, minced
- ¼ tsp sea salt
- Black pepper, to taste
- 3 tbsp red wine vinegar

- 1 tbsp apple cider vinegar
- ¼ cup fresh dill, chopped

How to prepare:
1. Add potatoes to a large saucepan and cover with water.
2. Bring it to boil, once done, let it simmer for 15 minutes.
3. Drain potatoes and let cool.
4. Add all ingredients to a bowl and mix it well.
5. Place in a serving dish and sever.

Preparation time: 10 minutes
Cooking time: 30 minutes
Total time: 40 minutes
Servings: 14

Nutritional Values:
- *Calories 80*
- *Total Fat 3 g*
- *Saturated Fat 0.4 g*
- *Cholesterol 0 mg*
- *Sodium 111.1 mg*
- *Total Carbs 12.2 g*
- *Fiber 1.6 g*
- *Sugar 0.8 g*
- *Protein 1.5 g*
- *Potassium 0 mg*

Kale Salad

Ingredients:

Vegetables:
- 4 large carrots, halved and roughly chopped
- 1 whole beet, tinly sliced
- 2 water (substitute avocado or melted coconut oil)
- 1 pinch sea salt

Dressing:
- 1/3 cup tahini
- 3 tbsp lemon juice
- 1-2 tbsp maple syrup
- 1 pinch sea salt
- ¼ cup water

Salad:
- 8 cups kale, roughly chopped
- ½ cup cherry tomatoes, chopped
- 1 ripe avocado, cubed

How to prepare:
1. Preheat oven to 375 F.
2. Line a baking dish with parchment paper.
3. Place carrots on the baking dish and bake them for 25 minutes.
4. Meanwhile, add all ingredients to a bowl and mix it all well.
5. Add the carrots, mix again, and serve in a serving dish.

Preparation time: 10 minutes
Cooking time: 40 minutes
Total time: 50 minutes
Servings: 4

Nutritional Values:
- *Calories 472*
- *Total Fat 22.8 g*
- *Saturated Fat 3.8 g*
- *Cholesterol 0 mg*
- *Sodium 214 mg*
- *Total Carbs 58.7 g*
- *Fiber 12.5 g*
- *Sugar 9.2 g*
- *Protein 14.6 g*
- *Potassium 0 mg*

Penne Pasta Salad

Ingredients:

Pasta salad:
- 2 cups cherry tomatoes, halved
- 12-ounce whole-grain or gluten-free penne pasta, cooked

Pesto:
- 2 cups fresh basil
- 4 cloves garlic, minced
- ¼ cup pine nuts, toasted
- 1 medium lemon, juiced
- ¼ cup vegan parmesan cheese
- 1 pinch sea salt

How to prepare:

1. Preheat oven to 400 F.
2. Line a baking sheet and line with parchment paper. Lay tomatoes on it.
3. Drizzle them with olive oil and bake tomatoes for 20 minutes.
4. Meanwhile, make the pesto by adding garlic, basil, pine nuts, cheese, and salt to a food processor and pulse it until smooth.
5. Now add all ingredients to a bowl.
6. Mix well and serve.

Preparation time: 10 minutes
Cooking time: 20 minutes
Total time: 30 minutes
Servings: 6

Nutritional Values:

- *Calories 352*
- *Total Fat 19.7 g*
- *Saturated Fat 2.7 g*
- *Cholesterol 0 mg*
- *Sodium 116 mg*
- *Total Carbs 37.3 g*
- *Fiber 1.6 g*
- *Sugar 1.6 g*
- *Protein 9.6 g*
- *Potassium 0 mg*

Niçoise Salad

Ingredients:

Salad:

- 6 small red or yellow potatoes, halved and boiled
- 1 cup green beans
- 1 head lettuce, chopped
- ½ cup pitted Nicoise, green, or kalamata olives
- ½ cup tomato, sliced

Chickpeas:

- 1 can chickpeas
- 1 tsp Dijon mustard

- 1 tsp Stevia
- 1 tsp dried dill
- 1 pinch sea salt
- 1 tbsp roasted unsalted sunflower seeds

Dressing:
- 1 heaping tsp Dijon mustard
- 1 tsp fresh thyme, chopped
- 1/3 cup white or red wine vinegar
- ¼ tsp each salt and pepper
- ¼ cup olive oil

How to prepare:
1. Add all ingredients to a large bowl and mix well to combine.
2. Serve and enjoy.

Preparation time: 15 minutes

Cooking time: 0 minutes

Total time: 15 minutes

Servings: 2

Nutritional Values:

- Calories 1,005
- Total Fat 32.9 g
- Saturated Fat 4.6 g
- Cholesterol 0 mg
- Sodium 1,259 mg
- Total Carbs 159.6 g
- Fiber 28.5 g
- Sugar 11.5 g
- Protein 23.5 g
- Potassium 3,275 mg

CHAPTER 4 «PASTA & NOODLES DISHES»

Rustic Pasta

Ingredients:

- 2 pints small tomatoes, sliced

- 3 tbsp + 1 tsp extra virgin olive oil, divided

- 1 small clove garlic, finely grated

- ¼ cup fresh basil leaves, sliced Sea salt, to taste

- Black pepper, to taste

- 1 cup chickpeas, cooked

- ¼ cup pine nuts, raw

- 1-2 tbsp nutritional yeast

- ¼ tsp garlic powder
- ½ tsp lemon zest
- 1 lb pasta, cooked

How to prepare:

1. Add tomatoes to a bowl.
2. Add in 3 tbsp of oil, the garlic, basil, olive oil, basil, salt, and pepper.
3. Cover the bowl and set it aside for 4 hours.
4. Preheat oven to 400 F.
5. Add chickpeas to a baking dish and toss them with the remaining oil, salt, and pepper.
6. Bake for 12 minutes.
7. Add in pine nuts and roast for another 6 minutes.
8. Take out and let them cool.
9. Add roasted chickpeas and pine nuts to a food processor.
10. Add in all remaining ingredients except, pasta, tomatoes, and roasted chickpeas and pine nut puree.
11. Pulse until mixture is crumbly.
12. Add pasta, roasted chickpeas and pine nut puree and tomatoes to a bowl.
13. Toss well and serve.

Preparation time: 20 minutes
Cooking time: 18 minutes

Total time: 38 minutes

Servings: 4

Nutritional Values:

- *Calories 678*
- *Total Fat 22.2 g*
- *Saturated Fat 2.6 g*
- *Cholesterol 83 mg*
- *Sodium 46 mg*
- *Total Carbs 97.5 g*
- *Fiber 10.5 g*
- *Sugar 7.3 g*
- *Protein 25.5 g*
- *Potassium 907 mg*

Vegan Lasagna

Ingredients:

ALMOND RICOTTA INGREDIENTS (makes extra):

- 2 cups sliced or slivered almonds, soaked in boiling water for 1 hour
- ½ cup reserved soaking water
- ½ tsp probiotic powder (loose or from a capsule)
- 1tbsp olive oil
- Sea salt, to taste

SPINACH WALNUT PESTO INGREDIENTS:

- ½ cup walnut halves

- 2 cloves garlic, finely minced
- ½ tsp lemon zest
- 1 tsp fresh lemon juice
- 2 cups spinach, packed
- 3 tbsp olive oil
- Sea salt and ground black pepper

LASAGNA INGREDIENTS:

- 1 tbsp olive oil
- 1 cup onion, diced
- ½ cup carrot, diced
- ½ cup zucchini, diced
- ⅓ cup French lentils, cooked
- 2 cloves garlic, finely minced
- ½ chili flakes
- Sea salt and ground black pepper
- 3 cups tomato sauce
- 6 oven-ready lasagna noodles (about 6-7 sheets), broken into thirds and boiled

How to prepare:

Almond Ricotta:

1. Add almonds to a food processor with ¼ cup water and pulse until slightly creamy.
2. Scrape it out into a glass container and let it ferment for 8 hours.

Pesto:

1. Roast walnuts for 5 minutes in a skillet over medium heat.
2. Transfer all pesto ingredients into a food processor and pulse until a sauce forms.
3. Transfer to a bowl.

Lasagna:

1. Add all lasagna ingredients except noodles and tomato sauce to a pan and sauté for 1 minute.
2. Add in tomato sauce and let it simmer.
3. Spread lasagna noodles in a saucepan and layer them with sauce, ricotta, and pesto.
4. Cover with the lid and cook for 10 minutes.

Serve and enjoy.

Preparation time: 20 minutes
Cooking time: 12 minutes
Total time: 32 minutes
Servings: 6

Nutritional Values:

- Calories 544
- Total Fat 33.2 g
- Saturated Fat 2.6 g
- Cholesterol 83 mg
- Sodium 661 mg
- Total Carbs 48.5 g
- Fiber 13.7 g
- Sugar 10 g
- Protein 21.3 g
- Potassium 1,073 mg

Garlic Alfredo Pasta

Ingredients:

Brussels sprouts:

- 16-ounce Brussels sprouts, halved
- 1-2 tbsp olive oil
- 1 pinch each sea salt and black pepper

Sauce + pasta:

- 3 tbsp olive oil or vegan butter
- 4 large cloves garlic, chopped
- 1/3 cup dry white wine
- 4 tbsp cornstarch
- ¾ cup unsweetened plain almond milk

- 4 tbsp nutritional yeast
- Sea salt and black pepper, to taste
- ¼ cup vegan parmesan cheese
- 10-ounce vegan, gluten-free pasta, cooked

How to prepare:

1. Preheat oven to 400 F.
2. Place Brussels sprouts on a baking sheet.
3. Drizzle with oil, salt, and pepper and toss.
4. Spread the sprouts in a single layer and set aside.
5. Now, to make the pasta sauce, add oil and garlic in a skillet over medium heat and sauté for 3 minutes.
6. Add in the wine and stir for 2 minutes.
7. Add cornstarch, almond milk, yeast, salt, pepper, and cheese and whisk continuously.
8. Bake Brussels sprouts for 15 minutes.
9. Once done, add pasta and Brussels sprouts to the skillet and mix them with the sauce.
10. Serve and enjoy.

Preparation time: 10 minutes
Cooking time: 20 minutes
Total time: 30 minutes
Servings: 4

Nutritional Values:

- *Calories 509*
- *Total Fat 18.5 g*
- *Saturated Fat 2.4 g*
- *Cholesterol 0 mg*
- *Sodium 450 mg*
- *Total Carbs 75.4 g*
- *Fiber 7.7 g*
- *Sugar 2.9 g*
- *Protein 12.4 g*
- *Potassium 410 mg*

Golden Pasta

Ingredients:

- ¼ cup extra virgin olive oil
- 1 sweet onion, chopped
- 6 cloves garlic, minced or grated
- 1 tbsp dried basil
- 1 tbsp dried oregano
- 2 tsp ground turmeric
- Kosher salt and pepper, to taste
- 1 (28-oz) can fire roasted tomatoes, crushed
- ½ cup oil-packed sundried tomatoes, oil drained and chopped

- 1 tbsp apple cider vinegar
- 1 (8-oz) box red lentil pasta or another short cut pasta, cooked
- 2 large handfuls baby spinach or kale
- Grated parmesan, nutritional yeast, toasted pine nuts and or seeds, for garnish

How to prepare:

1. Heat a large pot over medium heat.
2. Add oil and onions to the pot and cook for 5 minutes.
3. Add in garlic, basil, oregano, turmeric, salt, and pepper and cook for 1 minute.
4. Let it simmer for 15 minutes.
5. Add in spinach and cook for 5 minutes.
6. Add in pasta and cook for 1 more minute.
7. Serve and enjoy.

Preparation time: 10 minutes

Cooking time: 26 minutes

Total time: 36 minutes

Servings: 6

Nutritional Values:

- Calories 378
- Total Fat 11.5 g
- Saturated Fat 1.4 g
- Cholesterol 0 mg
- Sodium 94 mg
- Total Carbs 55.3 g
- Fiber 6.1 g
- Sugar 3.2 g
- Protein 16.3 g
- Potassium 271 mg

Creamy Spinach Pasta

Ingredients:

- 8 oz dry pasta, cooked
- 1-2 tbsp olive oil or buttery spread or oil spray
- 1½ tbsp garlic, minced
- 3 tbsp flour
- 1 tsp onion powder
- ½ tsp salt
- 1½ tsp dried oregano
- 1 cup cashew cream
- 1 cup unsweetened milk
- 1 can diced tomatoes

How to prepare:

1. Add garlic to a skillet and sauté for 1 minute.

2. Sauté for 1 minute.

3. Add in flour, onion powder, and salt and sauté for 1 more minute.

4. Add in cream, milk, oregano, and parmesan and bring to a boil, stirring constantly.

5. Whisk for a minute then add tomato in it.

6. Stir in pasta and combine well.

7. Serve and enjoy.

Preparation time: 10 minutes

Cooking time: 5 minutes

Total time: 15 minutes

Servings: 6

Nutritional Values:

- *Calories 210*
- *Total Fat 4 g*
- *Saturated Fat 1 g*
- *Cholesterol 0 mg*
- *Sodium 2 mg*
- *Total Carbs 30 g*
- *Fiber 0 g*
- *Sugar 2 g*
- *Protein 6 g*
- *Potassium 239 mg*

Basil Noodle Salad

Ingredients:

- 1/3 cup Simple Truth Tahini sesame seed paste
- 2 tbsp honey
- 1 lime, juice and zest
- 2 tbsp fish sauce
- 1 clove garlic, minced or grated
- 1 tbsp fresh ginger, grated
- 2 cups rice noodles, cooked
- 4 cups baby kale, finely chopped
- 2 cups frozen shelled edamame, thawed
- 3 carrots, shredded
- 2 bell peppers, sliced thin
- 1 cup fresh or frozen mango, chopped into chunks
- 2 stalks lemongrass, finely chopped

- 4 green onions, chopped
- ½ cup fresh basil
- ¼ cup cilantro
- Sliced Fresno peppers, sesame seeds, and roasted cashews, for garnish

How to prepare:
1. Add all ingredients except rice noodles to a large bowl.
2. Mix everything well.
3. Add in rice noodles and stir well.
4. Serve and enjoy.

Preparation time: 15 minutes

Cooking time: 5 minutes

Total time: 20 minutes

Servings: 6

Nutritional Values:
- *Calories 243*
- *Total Fat 6.1 g*
- *Saturated Fat 0.9 g*
- *Cholesterol 0 mg*
- *Sodium 514 mg*
- *Total Carbs 42.2 g*
- *Fiber 6.1 g*
- *Sugar 14.3 g*
- *Protein 8.9 g*
- *Potassium 485 mg*

Sweet Potato Noodles

Ingredients:

For the Ginger Tempeh:

- 1 8-oz package tempeh, cubed
- 2 garlic cloves, minced
- 2 tbsp maple syrup
- 2 tbsp soy sauce
- 1 tsp sesame oil
- 1 ½ tbsp vegetable oil, for frying

For the Crispy Kale:

- 4 kale leaves

- 1 tbsp olive oil or vegetable oil
- ¼ tsp salt

For the Sweet Potato Noodles:
- 2 sweet potatoes, peeled
- ½ cup coconut milk
- ½ tbsp maple syrup
- 1 tbsp soy sauce
- 1 tsp sesame oil
- 1 tsp Sriracha
- 1 tbsp vegetable oil, for pan-frying
- ¼ cup water

How to prepare:
1. Add garlic, maple syrup, soy sauce, and sesame oil to a bowl and stir well.
2. Add in tempeh and let marinate for 4 hours.
3. Preheat oven to 425 F and line a baking sheet with parchment paper.
4. Drizzle kale with olive oil and season with salt.
5. Bake for 10 minutes.
6. Take a spiralizer and spiralize the sweet potatoes into noodles and set aside.
7. For the sauce, add coconut milk, maple syrup, soy sauce, sesame oil, and sriracha to a saucepan and heat it on medium heat.
8. Let boil for 2 to 3 minutes.

9. Add vegetable oil to a large skillet.

10. Add the marinated tempeh to it and cook for 3 minutes on each side.

11. Add noodles and tempeh to the creamy sauce.

12. Stir in kale.

13. Stir well for a minute and serve.

Preparation time: 10 minutes
Cooking time: 15 minutes
Total time: 25 minutes
Servings: 2

Nutritional Values:

- *Calories 564*
- *Total Fat 41 g*
- *Saturated Fat 0 g*
- *Cholesterol 0 mg*
- *Sodium 1,993 mg*
- *Total Carbs 31 g*
- *Fiber 0 g*
- *Sugar 17 g*
- *Protein 23 g*
- *Potassium 102 mg*

Devilish Ramen

Ingredients:

- 2-inch piece ginger, cut into 3 slices
- 1 small onion, cut into ½-inch wedges
- 4 unpeeled garlic cloves
- 4 cups water
- 3 cups vegetable broth
- ¼ cup reduced-sodium tamari
- 1 tsp toasted sesame seed oil
- ½ tsp sea salt
- 1 10-oz package super-firm tofu, cut into ¼-inch slices
- 2 vegan sausages, cut into ¼-inch slices on the bias
- 2 tbsp sake or mirin

- ¼ small cabbage, chopped
- 1 small carrot, julienned
- 10 oz ramen noodles, cooked
- Scallions, minced
- Togarashi seasoning

How to prepare:

1. Heat a large pot over medium-high heat.
2. Add in ginger, onion, and garlic and cook for 3 minutes.
3. Add in water, broth, tamari, oil, doles, and salt and bring to boil.
4. Once boiled, let it simmer for 15 minutes.
5. Strain broth into a pot with the vegetables.
6. Add in tofu, sausage, and sake and continue to simmer.
7. Heat another large pot over medium heat and add in the cabbage.
8. Cook for about 5 minutes and combine everything in a bowl to serve with ramen.

Preparation time: 15 minutes
Cooking time: 20 minutes
Total time: 35 minutes
Servings: 2

Nutritional Values:

- *Calories 961*
- *Total Fat 33.8 g*
- *Saturated Fat 13.8 g*
- *Cholesterol 0 mg*
- *Sodium 5,336 mg*
- *Total Carbs 106.7 g*
- *Fiber 9.9 g*
- *Sugar 6.3 g*
- *Protein 44.3 g*
- *Potassium 1,203 mg*

Tofu Noodle Bowl

Ingredients:

For the Tofu Noodle Bowl:
- 1 (14-oz) block firm tofu, drained
- 1 cup onion, chopped
- ¾ cup bell pepper, chopped
- 2 cups vermicelli noodles, cooked

For the Marinade:
- 1 tbsp soy sauce or tamari
- ½ tbsp hot sauce
- ½ tbsp tahini
- 1 tbsp lime juice, freshly squeezed

- 1 tbsp sesame seed

For the Sauce:
- 2 tbsp soy sauce or tamari
- 1 tbsp hot sauce
- 1 tbsp tahini
- 2 tbsp lime juice, freshly squeezed

How to prepare:
1. Add all marinade ingredients except tofu to a bowl and mix well.
2. Slice tofu into cubes, place them on a baking sheet and top them with the marinade.
3. Set aside for 30 minutes.
4. Preheat oven to 400 F and bake tofu for 15 minutes.
5. Place noodles and bowl ingredients in a bowl and mix well.
6. Top with tofu and serve.

Preparation time: 30 minutes
Cooking time: 15 minutes
Total time: 45 minutes
Servings: 2

Nutritional Values:

- *Calories 488*
- *Total Fat 16.8 g*
- *Saturated Fat 2.9 g*
- *Cholesterol 0 mg*
- *Sodium 1680 mg*
- *Total Carbs 60.4 g*
- *Fiber 7.5 g*
- *Sugar 6.9 g*
- *Protein 28.7 g*
- *Potassium 622 mg*

Haka Noodles

Ingredients:

For the Noodles:
- 1 package haka noodles, cooked
- 1 large carrot, shredded or cut into thin matchsticks
- 1 bell pepper, thinly sliced
- 1 cup cabbage, shredded
- 1 cup French beans, sliced
- 1 cup tofu, drained, pressed, and cubed
- 1 small onion, thinly sliced
- 3-4 green onions, sliced
- 1 tsp red chili flakes
- 4 tbsp sesame oil

- 2 tbsp soy sauce
- 1 tbsp vinegar
- Salt, to taste

For the Sauce:

- 4 garlic cloves
- 1-inch piece ginger, finely grated
- 1 tbsp Sriracha sauce
- 2 tbsp tomato paste or ketchup
- 1 tbsp sesame seeds

How to prepare:

1. For the sauce, take all the sauce ingredients and blend them.
2. Add sesame oil and tofu to a skillet and cook over medium heat until tofu is browned on both sides.
3. Take out tofu, add in chilies, and onions and cook for 3 minutes.
4. Add in tomato paste and cook for 2 minutes.
5. Add soy sauce and vinegar and lower the heat.
6. Add in all the vegetables and cook for an additional 3 minutes.
7. Add in noodles, stir well and serve.

Preparation time: 10 minutes

Cooking time: 20 minutes

Total time: 30 minutes

Servings: 4

Nutritional Values:

- *Calories 661*
- *Total Fat 21 g*
- *Saturated Fat 0 g*
- *Cholesterol 0 mg*
- *Sodium 789 mg*
- *Total Carbs 93 g*
- *Fiber 0 g*
- *Sugar 9 g*
- *Protein 23 g*
- *Potassium 0 mg*

CHAPTER 5 «STIR-FRIED, GRILLED & HASHED VEGETABLES RECIPES»

Veggie Stir Fry

Ingredients:

- 5 garlic cloves, finely minced
- ½ red onion, sliced in thin strips
- 1 (8-oz) package mini sweet peppers, cut into thin rings (seeded)
- 2 carrots, peeled and cut into thin slivers
- 1 celery stalk, diced
- 3 broccoli heads, cut into cubes
- 1 can water chestnuts, drained

94

- ½ cup teriyaki sauce
- 2 tbsp tamari
- 2 tsp cornstarch
- 2 tbsp sesame seeds

How to prepare:
1. Heat a large skillet over medium heat.
2. Add all ingredients to the skillet and stir well.
3. Cook for 4 minutes.
4. Serve with anything you like.

Preparation time: 10 minutes
Cooking time: 4 minutes
Total time: 14 minutes
Servings: 5

Nutritional Values:
- *Calories 103*
- *Total Fat 2.1 g*
- *Saturated Fat 0.3 g*
- *Cholesterol 0 mg*
- *Sodium 1,559 mg*
- *Total Carbs 16.8 g*
- *Fiber 3.4 g*
- *Sugar 8 g*
- *Protein 5.7 g*
- *Potassium 385 mg*

Brown Rice Stir Fry

Ingredients:

- ½ cup uncooked brown rice, cooked
- 1 cup red cabbage, chopped
- 1 cup broccoli, chopped
- ½ red bell pepper, chopped
- ½ zucchini, chopped
- 2 tbsp extra virgin olive oil
- 4 cloves of garlic, minced
- 1 handful fresh parsley, finely chopped
- 1/8 tsp cayenne powder
- 2 tbsp tamari or soy sauce

How to prepare:

1. Add some water to a frying pan and bring it to boil.

2. Add in the veggies and cook for 2 minutes on high heat.

3. Drain veggies and set aside.

4. Add olive oil, garlic, parsley, and cayenne and cook for 2 minutes.

5. Add in rice and drained vegetables and cook for 1 minute.

6. Serve and enjoy.

Preparation time: 10 minutes

Cooking time: 15 minutes

Total time: 25 minutes

Servings: 4

Nutritional Values:
- *Calories 179*
- *Total Fat 7.9 g*
- *Saturated Fat 1.2 g*
- *Cholesterol 0 mg*
- *Sodium 522 mg*
- *Total Carbs 24.5 g*
- *Fiber 2.7 g*
- *Sugar 2.4 g*
- *Protein 4.5 g*
- *Potassium 330 mg*

Teriyaki Stir Fry

Ingredients:
- 1 cup jasmine rice, cooked
- 12 oz package frozen shelled edamame
- 6 small sweet red peppers, chopped
- 1 onion, chopped
- 1 small head broccoli, chopped
- 1 cup carrots, shredded
- 2 cloves garlic, minced
- 2 tsp ground ginger
- Salt & pepper, to taste
- 4 stalks green onion, chopped for garnish
- Sprinkle of sesame seeds, for garnish

- Few splashes vegetable broth, for finishing
- Few dollops homemade teriyaki sauce, for garnish

How to prepare:

1. Add red peppers, onions, broccoli and carrots to a saucepan and sauté for 5 minutes over medium heat.
2. Stir in all the remaining ingredients and sauté for about 3 minutes.
3. Serve with jasmine rice and enjoy.

Preparation time: 10 minutes
Cooking time: 14 minutes
Total time: 24 minutes
Servings: 5

Nutritional Values:

- *Calories 292*
- *Total Fat 4.1 g*
- *Saturated Fat 0.4 g*
- *Cholesterol 0 mg*
- *Sodium 35 mg*
- *Total Carbs 53.5 g*
- *Fiber 7.6 g*
- *Sugar 11.3 g*
- *Protein 12.4 g*
- *Potassium 807 mg*

Hot Grilled Watermelon

Ingredients:

- 1 small red watermelon, sliced into quarters
- 2 lemons, juiced
- ¾ tsp kosher salt

How to prepare:

1. Preheat oven to 500 F.
2. Pour lemon juice and sprinkle salt on watermelon.
3. Grill watermelon slices for 1 minute on each side.
4. Serve and enjoy.

Preparation time: 10 minutes
Cooking time: 10 minutes

Total time: 20 minutes

Servings: 10

Nutritional Values:

- *Calories 106*
- *Total Fat 0.5 g*
- *Saturated Fat 0.2 g*
- *Cholesterol 0 mg*
- *Sodium 179 mg*
- *Total Carbs 26.9 g*
- *Fiber 1.7 g*
- *Sugar 21.4 g*
- *Protein 2.2 g*
- *Potassium 398 mg*

Grilled Mushrooms

Ingredients:

- 2 lb mushrooms, sliced ¼-inch thick
- 2 tbsp balsamic vinegar
- 1 tbsp soy sauce
- 3 cloves garlic, chopped
- ½ tsp thyme, chopped
- Salt and pepper, to taste

How to prepare:

1. Mix balsamic vinegar, soy sauce, garlic, thyme, salt, and pepper in a bowl to make a marinade.
2. Marinate mushrooms in the marinade for 30 minutes.
3. Grill mushrooms over medium heat for 3 minutes on each side.

4. Serve and enjoy.

Preparation time: 40 minutes

Cooking time: 10 minutes

Total time: 50 minutes

Servings: 4

Nutritional Values:

- *Calories 56*
- *Total Fat 0.7 g*
- *Saturated Fat 0 g*
- *Cholesterol 0 mg*
- *Sodium 239 mg*
- *Total Carbs 8.7 g*
- *Fiber 2.4 g*
- *Sugar 4 g*
- *Protein 7.5 g*
- *Potassium 746 mg*

Grilled Tofu

Ingredients:

- 1 block firm or extra-firm tofu
- 1 tbsp mustard
- 3 tbsp BBQ dry rub
- ¼ cup barbecue sauce

How to prepare:

1. Add all ingredients except tofu to a bowl and mix them.
2. Toss tofu in it to coat liberally.
3. Grill tofu on a grill that is around 250 degrees F.
4. Cook for about 30 minutes.
5. Serve and enjoy.

Preparation time: 10 minutes

Cooking time: 30 minutes

Total time: 40 minutes

Servings: 2

Nutritional Values:

- *Calories 115*
- *Total Fat 4.4 g*
- *Saturated Fat 0.3 g*
- *Cholesterol 0 mg*
- *Sodium 624 mg*
- *Total Carbs 14.2 g*
- *Fiber 1.2 g*
- *Sugar 8.8 g*
- *Protein 5.9 g*
- *Potassium 163 mg*

Grilled Pineapple

Ingredients:

- 1 tsp melted coconut oil
- 5 cups pineapple, cut into ½- inch circles
- 1 tsp cinnamon

How to prepare:

1. Heat grill to a high temperature.
2. Brush grill with coconut oil.
3. Grill pineapple for 5 minutes on each side.
4. Sprinkle cinnamon on top.
5. Serve and enjoy.

Preparation time: 10 minutes

Cooking time: 10 minutes

Total time: 20 minutes

Servings: 6

Nutritional Values:

- *Calories 76*
- *Total Fat 0.9 g*
- *Saturated Fat 0.7 g*
- *Cholesterol 0 mg*
- *Sodium 2 mg*
- *Total Carbs 18.4 g*
- *Fiber 2.1 g*
- *Sugar 13.6 g*
- *Protein 0.8 g*
- *Potassium 152 mg*

Sweet Potato Hash

Ingredients:

- 1 small onion, diced
- 1 sweet potato, diced into ½-inch cubes
- ¼–½ cup orange juice or low-sodium vegetable broth
- 1 tbsp almond butter
- ½ tsp cinnamon
- ½ tsp chili powder
- Pinch red pepper flakes, or more to taste
- ½ bunch kale, shredded

How to prepare:

1. Heat a skillet and add onion and potatoes to it.
2. Sauté for 3 minutes.

3. Add in remaining ingredients and stir for 5 minutes.

4. Let it simmer for 3 more minutes.

5. Serve and enjoy.

Preparation time: 9 minutes

Cooking time: 11 minutes

Total time: 20 minutes

Servings: 2

Nutritional Values:

- *Calories 134*
- *Total Fat 4.8 g*
- *Saturated Fat 0.4 g*
- *Cholesterol 0 mg*
- *Sodium 71 mg*
- *Total Carbs 19.7 g*
- *Fiber 4.3 g*
- *Sugar 5.6 g*
- *Protein 4.9 g*
- *Potassium 481 mg*

Veggie Breakfast Hash

Ingredients:
- 4 cups potatoes, peeled and cubed
- Salt and pepper, to taste
- 1 can pinto beans, drained and rinsed
- 1 cup zucchini, chopped
- 1 cup squash, chopped
- 1 red bell pepper, chopped
- ½ cup mushrooms, sliced
- 1½ tsp garlic powder
- 1½ tsp onion powder
- ½ tsp paprika
- Pinch of chili flakes

How to prepare:
1. Preheat the oven to 425 degrees F.

2. Place potatoes on a baking sheet and line it with parchment paper.
3. Bake potatoes for 25 minutes by placing the dish in the oven.
4. Take out the baking dish and add in the beans, zucchini, squash, bell peppers, mushrooms.
5. Sprinkle with the seasonings and bake for about 15 minutes.
6. Remove from the oven and take a large bowl.
7. Dump everything in the bowl and mix well.
8. Serve and have fun!

Preparation time: 10 minutes
Cooking time: 40 minutes
Total time: 50 minutes
Servings: 4

Nutritional Values:
- *Calories 295*
- *Total Fat 1 g*
- *Saturated Fat 0.2 g*
- *Cholesterol 0 mg*
- *Sodium 20 mg*
- *Total Carbs 59.1 g*
- *Fiber 12.2 g*
- *Sugar 5.5 g*
- *Protein 14.2 g*
- *Potassium 1,488 mg*

Tempeh Bacon Hash

Ingredients:

Tempeh Bacon:
- 1 block tempeh, sliced into very thin strips
- 1 tbsp grapeseed oil
- 1 tbsp pure maple syrup
- 2 tsp smoked paprika
- 1 tsp chipotle powder
- ½ tsp cumin

Hash:
- 1-2 tbsp grapeseed oil

- 1 onion, diced
- 2 medium sweet potatoes, chopped
- 1 red bell pepper, chopped
- 1 portobello mushroom cap, chopped
- 1 tbsp dried oregano
- ¼ cup nutritional yeast
- 2 cloves garlic, minced
- 1 heaping cup fresh kale, chopped
- ¼ cup fresh basil, chopped

How to prepare:

1. For bacon, lay tempeh slices on a baking dish.
2. In a bowl, add remaining tempeh ingredients and drizzle that over the sliced tempeh.
3. Let marinade for 15 minutes.
4. Heat a skillet and Cook tempeh slices for 3 minutes on each side.
5. Take out tempeh and chop the slices.
6. For hash, add all hash ingredients to a skillet over medium heat and cook for 12 minutes.
7. Add in tempeh and cook for 3 more minutes.
8. Serve and enjoy.

Preparation time: 15 minutes
Cooking time: 25 minutes

Total time: 40 minutes

Servings: 4

Nutritional Values:

- *Calories 278*
- *Total Fat 12.4 g*
- *Saturated Fat 1.8 g*
- *Cholesterol 0 mg*
- *Sodium 25 mg*
- *Total Carbs 35.5 g*
- *Fiber 4.9 g*
- *Sugar 5.7 g*
- *Protein 9.9 g*
- *Potassium 892 mg*

CHAPTER 6 «DESSERTS & SNACKS RECIPES»

Strawberry Mango Shave Ice

Ingredients:

- ½ cup superfine sugar, divided

- 1-quart strawberries, diced

- 1½ cups mango juice

- 1 mango, diced

- ½ cup coconut, toasted

How to prepare:

1. Add 1 cup water and ¾ cup sugar to a pot and boil over medium heat.

2. Once boiled, remove from heat and add 2 more cups of water.
3. Freeze this mixture stirring after every 45 minutes.
4. Take a blender and add all remaining ingredients and blend until smooth.
5. Strain the mixture into a container with a pour spout.
6. For serving, divide the ice into glasses and pour juice and mixture over them.
7. Serve and enjoy.

Preparation time: 5 hours 30 minutes
Cooking time: 0 minutes
Total time: 5 hours 30 minutes
Servings: 3

Nutritional Values:
- *Calories 366*
- *Total Fat 5.5 g*
- *Saturated Fat 4.1 g*
- *Cholesterol 0 mg*
- *Sodium 31 mg*
- *Total Carbs 82.4 g*
- *Fiber 6.8 g*
- *Sugar 74.4 g*
- *Protein 2.7 g*
- *Potassium 529 mg*

Chocolate Avocado Mousse

Ingredients:

- 1¼ cups almond milk, unsweetened
- 1 lb dairy-free dark chocolate (preferably 60% cacao), coarsely chopped
- 4 small ripe avocados, pitted, peeled, and chopped
- ¼ cup agave syrup
- 1 tbsp orange zest, finely grated
- 2 tbsp puffed quinoa
- 2 tsp Maldon sea salt
- 2 tsp Aleppo pepper flakes
- 1 tbsp extra virgin olive oil

How to prepare:

1. Heat almond milk in a saucepan. After 5 to 10 minutes, add in chopped chocolate.
2. Take all remaining ingredients and blend them until smooth.
3. Mix both and let cool for a while.
4. Refrigerate for about 2 hours before serving.

Preparation time: 10 minutes

Cooking time: 10 minutes

Total time: 20 minutes

Servings: 6

Nutritional Values:

- Calories 540
- Total Fat 43.5 g
- Saturated Fat 27.5 g
- Cholesterol 0 mg
- Sodium 820 mg
- Total Carbs 61.2 g
- Fiber 11.4 g
- Sugar 1.7 g
- Protein 6.1 g
- Potassium 151 mg

Fudge

Ingredients:

- 1 cup vegan chocolate chips
- ½ cup soy milk

How to prepare:

1. Line an 8-inch portion skillet with wax paper. Set aside. Clear some space in your refrigerator for this dish as you will need it later.
2. Melt chocolate chips in a double boiler or add chocolate and almond spread to a medium, microwave-safe bowl. Melt it in the microwave in 20-second increments until

chocolate melts. In between each 20-second burst, stir the chocolate until it is smooth.

3. Empty the melted chocolate mixture into the lined skillet. Tap the sides of the skillet to make sure the mixture spreads into an even layer. Alternatively, use a spoon to make swirls on top.

4. Move skillet to the refrigerator until it is firm. Remove the skillet from the refrigerator and cut fudge into 18 squares.

Preparation time: 10 minutes
Cooking time: 5 minutes
Total time: 15 minutes
Servings: 18 pieces

Nutritional Values:

- *Calories 21*
- *Total Fat 1.2 g*
- *Saturated Fat 0.6 g*
- *Cholesterol 1 mg*
- *Sodium 2 mg*
- *Total Carbs 2.2 g*
- *Fiber 0.2 g*
- *Sugar 2 g*
- *Protein 0.2 g*
- *Potassium 8 mg*

Chocolate Chip Cookies

Ingredients:

- 1½ cups roasted, salted cashews
- 8 oz pitted Medjool dates, make sure you are using moist, plump dates
- 3 tbsp coconut oil
- 2 tsp vanilla extract
- 2 cups old-fashioned oats
- 1 cup semi-sweet or dark chocolate chips

How to prepare:

1. Line a baking sheet with parchment paper.
2. In the bowl of a food processor, add the cashews, dates, coconut oil, vanilla, and oats.
3. Pulse until combined, and all lumps are broken up.

4. On the off chance that the batter appears to be dry, add 1 more tbsp of coconut oil and a sprinkle of water. Mix in the chocolate chips.

5. Divide the mixture into 18 to 20 tbsp-size balls and place them on the prepared baking sheet. Using the palm of your hand, delicately press down each ball into flat circles. Move the sheet to the refrigerator for 10 to 15 minutes or until cookies are firm.

6. Serve and enjoy.

Preparation time: 20 minutes
Cooking time: 0 minutes
Total time: 20 minutes
Servings: 20 cookies

Nutritional Values:
- *Calories 207*
- *Total Fat 9.4 g*
- *Saturated Fat 3.9 g*
- *Cholesterol 0 mg*
- *Sodium 4 mg*
- *Total Carbs 28.1 g*
- *Fiber 2.7 g*
- *Sugar 12.2 g*
- *Protein 4.2 g*
- *Potassium 128 mg*

Peanut Butter Ice Cream

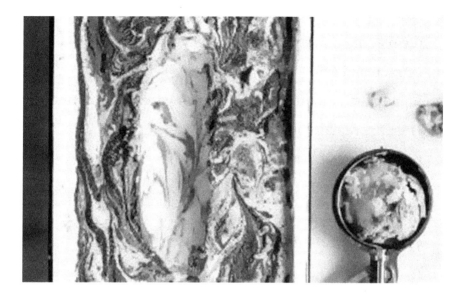

Note: This recipe calls for the use of a frozen yogurt or ice cream machine.

Ingredients:

- 1 cup dark chocolate chips
- 3 cans coconut cream, divided
- ¼ cup peanut butter
- ½ cup granulated sugar
- 2 tsp vanilla extract
- ¼ tsp salt
- ¼ cup graham cracker crumbs

How to prepare:

1. Reserve ½ cup of the coconut cream and add the rest to the blender along with peanut butter, sugar, vanilla extract, and salt.

2. Blend until smooth and freeze the mixture for 2 hours.

3. Heat the remaining ½ cup of the coconut cream in a small pot over low heat until it starts to boil.

4. Remove the pot from the heat and add the chocolate chips to the coconut cream.

5. Let this sit for 5 minutes then stir the mixture to combine the chocolate and the cream. The chocolate chips should be completely softened by this point.

6. Let the mixture cool to room temperature.

7. Meanwhile, take out the frozen mixture and mix with the coconut cream chocolate mixture and graham cracker crumbs in a bowl.

8. Let cool for 8 hours in the refrigerator.

9. Scoop out and serve chilled.

Preparation time: 20 minutes

Cooking time: 8 hours

Total time: 8 hours 20 minutes

Servings: 20

Nutritional Values:

- *Calories 154*
- *Total Fat 11.9 g*
- *Saturated Fat 9 g*
- *Cholesterol 0 mg*
- *Sodium 61 mg*
- *Total Carbs 12.5 g*
- *Fiber 1.1 g*
- *Sugar 10 g*
- *Protein 2.1 g*
- *Potassium 116 mg*

Cashew Cream Cheese

Ingredients:

- 1 cup raw cashews, soaked overnight
- 2-3 tbsp water
- ¼ cup lemon juice
- ½ tsp apple cider vinegar
- 2 tbsp nutritional yeast
- Salt, to taste

How to prepare:

1. Wash soaked cashews in a colander then transfer them to a blender or food processor and blend them with 2 to 3 tbsp of water until smooth.

2. Add in the rest of the ingredients and mix until combined.
3. If you'd like a vegetable cream "cheese," add chopped herbs, chives, peppers, carrots, and onions to the mixture.

Preparation time: 10 minutes
Cooking time: 0 minutes
Total time: 10 minutes
Servings: 6

Nutritional Values:
- *Calories 146*
- *Total Fat 10.8 g*
- *Saturated Fat 2.2 g*
- *Cholesterol 0 mg*
- *Sodium 8 mg*
- *Total Carbs 9.2 g*
- *Fiber 1.6 g*
- *Sugar 1.4 g*
- *Protein 5.1 g*
- *Potassium 223 mg*

Coconut Yogurt Chia Pudding

Ingredients:

- ½ cup vanilla coconut yogurt
- 2 tbsp chia seeds
- 3 tbsp almond milk

How to prepare:

1. Mix all ingredients in a bowl until well combined.
2. Place in the freezer for an hour or overnight.
3. When thickened, top with your favorite garnishes and serve.

Preparation time: 5 minutes
Cooking time: 0 minutes

Total time: 5 minutes

Servings: 1

Nutritional Values:

- *Calories 202*
- *Total Fat 15.5 g*
- *Saturated Fat 12.7 g*
- *Cholesterol 0 mg*
- *Sodium 9 mg*
- *Total Carbs 15.4 g*
- *Fiber 3.9 g*
- *Sugar 11 g*
- *Protein 2.7 g*
- *Potassium 156 mg*

Cinnamon Apples

Ingredients:

- 2 apples
- 1 tsp cinnamon

How to prepare:

1. Pre-heat stove to 220 degrees F.
2. Core the apples or cut them into rounds with a sharp blade or mandolin slicer.
3. Place them in a bowl and sprinkle them with cinnamon. Use your hands to make sure the apples are coated completely.

4. Arrange the apple cuts in a single layer on a silicone tray or a baking sheet lined with parchment paper.
5. Bake for 1 hour then flip the apples.
6. Bake for 1 more hour. Then, turn the oven off and leave the sheet in the stove until cooled.
7. Serve when desired or store in a sealed container for up to a week.

Preparation time: 20 minutes
Cooking time: 60 minutes
Total time: 1 hour 20 minutes
Servings: 4

Nutritional Values:

- *Calories 33*
- *Total Fat 0.1 g*
- *Saturated Fat 0 g*
- *Cholesterol 0 mg*
- *Sodium 1 mg*
- *Total Carbs 9.1 g*
- *Fiber 2.3 g*
- *Sugar 5.8 g*
- *Protein 0.2 g*
- *Potassium 67 mg*

Roasted Chickpeas

Ingredients:

- 1 can chickpeas, rinsed and drained
- 2 tsp freshly squeezed lemon juice
- 2 tsp tamari
- ½ tsp fresh rosemary, chopped
- 1/8 tsp sea salt
- 1/8 tsp pure maple syrup or agave nectar

How to prepare:

1. Preheat stove to 400°F (205°C). Line a baking sheet with parchment paper.
2. Toss all ingredients together and spread the chickpeas out on the baking sheet.

3. Roast for around 25 minutes, stirring the chickpeas every 5 minutes or so. Note, until the tamari and lemon juice dry up, the chickpeas will seem delicate, not crunchy.

4. Serve warm or at room temperature for a snack.

Preparation time: 10 minutes
Cooking time: 25 minutes
Total time: 35 minutes
Servings: 4

Nutritional Values:

- *Calories 290*
- *Total Fat 10.2 g*
- *Saturated Fat 1.5 g*
- *Cholesterol 0 mg*
- *Sodium 155 mg*
- *Total Carbs 40.3 g*
- *Fiber 10.4 g*
- *Sugar 6.2 g*
- *Protein 10.9 g*
- *Potassium 469 mg*

Baked Sesame Fries

Ingredients:

- 1 lb Yukon gold potatoes, unpeeled and cut into wedges
- 1 tbsp avocado, grapeseed, or sunflower oil (can use another medium-high heat oil if you prefer)
- 2 tbsp sesame seeds
- 1 tbsp potato starch (optional, but makes fries extra crispy)
- 1 tbsp nutritional yeast, optional
- Generous pinch salt, to taste
- Black pepper, to taste

How to prepare:

1. Preheat stove to 425 degrees F.
2. Delicately oil a metal baking sheet or line it with parchment paper.
3. Toss potatoes with all of the ingredients until covered, if seeds don't stick, drizzle a little more oil.
4. Spread potatoes onto the prepared sheet in an even layer (the more space between the wedges the better) and bake for 20 to 25 minutes, flipping once halfway through, until potatoes are crispy.
5. Serve immediately with desired toppings.

Preparation time: 10 minutes
Cooking time: 20 minutes
Total time: 30 minutes
Servings: 4

Nutritional Values:

- *Calories 192*
- *Total Fat 5.9 g*
- *Saturated Fat 0.6 g*
- *Cholesterol 0 mg*
- *Sodium 9 mg*
- *Total Carbs 32.6 g*
- *Fiber 2 g*
- *Sugar 0.3 g*
- *Protein 2.8 g*
- *Potassium 262 mg*

CHAPTER 7 «HOMEMADE BASICS, SAUCES & CONDIMENTS RECIPES»

Homemade Dip Sauce

Ingredients:

- 1 tbsp cashew cream
- 1 tbsp date syrup
- 1 tbsp ketchup
- 1 red onion
- 1 tbsp pickles
- 1 tbsp apple cider vinegar

- 1 tbsp sea salt
- 1 tbsp garlic powder
- 1 tbsp onion powder

How to prepare:

1. Take all the ingredients and blend in a food processor until smooth.
2. Serve and enjoy.

Preparation time: 10 minutes

Cooking time: 0 minutes

Total time: 10 minutes

Servings: 8

Nutritional Values:

- *Calories 19*
- *Total Fat 0.2 g*
- *Saturated Fat 0 g*
- *Cholesterol 0 mg*
- *Sodium 739 mg*
- *Total Carbs 4.2 g*
- *Fiber 0.5 g*
- *Sugar 2.4 g*
- *Protein 0.5 g*
- *Potassium 49 mg*

Roasted Red Pepper Hummus

Ingredients:

- 1 cup cooked chickpeas
- ¼ cup roasted red peppers + splash of juice from the jar or water
- 1 tbsp tahini
- ¼ tsp cumin
- ¼ tsp chili powder
- ½ tsp salt
- Pinch pepper

How to prepare:

1. Add all ingredients to a blender or food processor.
2. Make sure to scrape down the sides in the middle of blending to ensure that everything is mixed.

3. Once smooth, add salt or pepper or other spices to taste.
4. Refrigerate before serving if you prefer chilled hummus.
5. When ready to serve, transfer the hummus to a small bowl and garnish as desired.
6. Refrigerate any remaining hummus in a sealed container. It should be kept for 3 to 5 days but always check for freshness.

Preparation time: 5 minutes
Cooking time: 5 minutes
Total time: 10 minutes
Servings: 3

Nutritional Values:

- *Calories 273*
- *Total Fat 6.8 g*
- *Saturated Fat 0.8 g*
- *Cholesterol 0 mg*
- *Sodium 448 mg*
- *Total Carbs 43.7 g*
- *Fiber 12.4 g*
- *Sugar 7.8 g*
- *Protein 13.9 g*
- *Potassium 637 mg*

Nacho "Cheese"

Ingredients:

- 2 cups russet potatoes, peeled and chopped
- 1 cup carrots, chopped
- ½ cup water
- 1 tbsp lemon juice
- ½ cup nutritional yeast
- ½ tsp onion powder
- ½ tsp garlic powder
- 1 tsp salt
- ¼ cup salsa

How to prepare:

1. Boil potatoes and carrots for 10 minutes or until delicate. Drain the water.

2. Put potatoes, carrots, water, lemon juice, yeast, onion powder, garlic powder, salt, and salsa in a blender.
3. Mix until totally smooth then serve.

Preparation time: 10 minutes
Cooking time: 10 minutes
Total time: 20 minutes
Servings: 4

Nutritional Values:
- *Calories 141*
- *Total Fat 1.2 g*
- *Saturated Fat 0.2 g*
- *Cholesterol 0 mg*
- *Sodium 716 mg*
- *Total Carbs 25.2 g*
- *Fiber 7.9 g*
- *Sugar 3 g*
- *Protein 11.1 g*
- *Potassium 933 mg*

Bechamel Sauce

Ingredients:

- 3 tbsp vegan butter
- 2 tbsp flour
- 2 cups non-dairy milk, warmed
- Salt and pepper, to taste

How to prepare:

1. Melt butter in a pan over medium heat. Add flour and whisk until thickened and bubbling making sure it doesn't burn (roughly 2 minutes).
2. Pour warm milk into the skillet and keep on whisking until sauce is thick (roughly 3 minutes).
3. Add salt, pepper to the skillet and mix well.

4. Use quickly as desired. If making ahead of time (same day), place wax paper over the sauce until ready to use.

Preparation time: 5 minutes
Cooking time: 10 minutes
Total time: 15 minutes
Servings: 4 cups

Nutritional Values:
- *Calories 110*
- *Total Fat 6.1 g*
- *Saturated Fat 1.2 g*
- *Cholesterol 0 mg*
- *Sodium 77 mg*
- *Total Carbs 9.4 g*
- *Fiber 0.9 g*
- *Sugar 4.4 g*
- *Protein 3.9 g*
- *Potassium 5 mg*

Caramel Sauce

Ingredients:

- 2 tbsp almond butter
- 1 tbsp maple syrup, rice syrup, or agave syrup
- 1 tsp water

How to prepare:

1. Whisk together the almond spread, syrup, and water until smooth.
2. Let it sit for a couple of minutes to thicken up, then serve as desired.

Preparation time: 10 minutes

Cooking time: 0 minutes

Total time: 10 minutes

Servings: 2

Nutritional Values:

- *Calories 130*
- *Total Fat 9 g*
- *Saturated Fat 0.7 g*
- *Cholesterol 0 mg*
- *Sodium 8 mg*
- *Total Carbs 11.4 g*
- *Fiber 1.6 g*
- *Sugar 0.7 g*
- *Protein 3.4 g*
- *Potassium 126 mg*

Tzatziki

Ingredients:

- 1 cup plain vegan yogurt
- ¼ cucumber, grated
- 1 tbsp fresh dill
- 1 tsp lemon zest
- 1 tbsp nutritional yeast
- 1 tsp black pepper
- 1 tsp salt
- 1 clove garlic, minced
- 1 tbsp olive oil
- 1 tbsp lemon juice

How to prepare:

1. Combine all ingredients in a medium-sized bowl.

2. Stir to combine.

3. Pour into a serving dish, mix well, and refrigerate for 1 hour before serving.

Preparation time: 5 minutes
Cooking time: 0 minutes
Total time: 5 minutes
Servings: 4

Nutritional Values:
- *Calories 90*
- *Total Fat 6 g*
- *Saturated Fat 0.6 g*
- *Cholesterol 0 mg*
- *Sodium 589 mg*
- *Total Carbs 7.8 g*
- *Fiber 1 g*
- *Sugar 2.9 g*
- *Protein 2.6 g*
- *Potassium 129 mg*

Mayonnaise

Ingredients:

- 10.5 oz silken tofu
- 2 tbsp lemon juice
- 2 tbsp apple cider vinegar
- 1 tsp maple syrup
- ½ tsp salt
- 1 tsp mustard powder, or Dijon mustard
- 2 tbsp olive oil

How to prepare:

1. Blend all ingredients except mustard powder and olive oil until smooth.

2. Add mustard powder ¼ tsp at a time, mixing to combine after each addition. Taste as you go and stop adding the powder when you reach your desired flavor.
4. With the blender or food processor running, pour in the olive oil and mix until combined and shiny.
5. Store in a sealed container in the refrigerator.

Preparation time: 5 minutes
Cooking time: 0 minutes
Total time: 5 minutes
Servings: 2 cups

Nutritional Values:
- *Calories 229*
- *Total Fat 18.3 g*
- *Saturated Fat 2.7 g*
- *Cholesterol 0 mg*
- *Sodium 667 mg*
- *Total Carbs 6.4 g*
- *Fiber 0.3 g*
- *Sugar 4.3 g*
- *Protein 10.5 g*
- *Potassium 329 mg*

Homemade Ketchup

Ingredients:

- 7 oz tomato paste (salt-free)
- 2 tbsp raw apple cider vinegar
- ½ tsp liquid smoke
- ¼ tsp onion powder
- ¼ tsp garlic powder
- ¼ tsp smoked paprika
- 1/8 tsp cinnamon

How to prepare:

1. Mix all the ingredients until well combined.
2. Store in a hermetically sealed glass container or jug in the refrigerator for up to 14 days.

Preparation time: 5 minutes

Cooking time: 0 minutes

Total time: 5 minutes

Servings: 1 cup

Nutritional Values:
- *Calories 176*
- *Total Fat 1 g*
- *Saturated Fat 0.2 g*
- *Cholesterol 0 mg*
- *Sodium 197 mg*
- *Total Carbs 39.3 g*
- *Fiber 8.6 g*
- *Sugar 24.7 g*
- *Protein 8.8 g*
- *Potassium 2,061 mg*

Harissa Paste

Ingredients:

- 1 chargrilled capsicum
- 1 tsp coriander seeds
- 1 tsp caraway seeds
- 1 tsp chili flakes
- 1 tsp smoked paprika
- 2 tsp cumin seeds
- ½ tsp salt
- 1 tbsp tomato paste
- 4 tbsp extra virgin olive oil, or vegetable oil of your choice

How to prepare:

1. Dry toast the coriander, caraway, and cumin seeds in a small frying pan until fragrant, stirring them continuously.
2. Grind the seeds with a mortar and pestle or use a coffee grinder. If you have neither, you can leave the seeds whole without affecting the flavor of the paste.
3. Add everything to a blender or food processor and blend until smooth. Taste the paste and adjust the flavor as you like.
4. Scrape completed harissa paste into a sealed container and store in the refrigerator. You can drizzle a little bit of oil on top to extend the life of the paste.

Preparation time: 5 minutes
Cooking time: 5 minutes
Total time: 10 minutes
Servings: 1 cup

Nutritional Values:

- *Calories 606*
- *Total Fat 64.5 g*
- *Saturated Fat 9 g*
- *Cholesterol 0 mg*
- *Sodium 1863 mg*
- *Total Carbs 11.9 g*
- *Fiber 2.7 g*
- *Sugar 7 g*
- *Protein 3 g*
- *Potassium 321 mg*

Mint Chutney

Ingredients:

- 2-3 green chilies, seeded if desired
- ½ cup packed fresh mint leaves
- ½ cup packed cilantro
- ¼ tsp salt
- ¼ tsp sugar
- 2 tsp or more lemon juice
- ½ tsp apple cider or white vinegar or use more lemon juice
- 2 small cloves garlic, optional
- ½-inch piece ginger, optional
- ¼ cup water

How to prepare:

1. Blend everything until smooth. Taste and alter salt, zest, and lemon based on your preferences. Add more chilies for flavor if necessary and mix once more.

2. Refrigerate for up to 5 days. This can be frozen for 3 months in a sealed container. Defrost and use it when desired.

3. You can include a tbsp of nondairy yogurt, peanuts or coconut drops to make a thicker chutney. Adding in the optional garlic or ginger can make a garlic-mint chutney and a ginger-mint chutney respectively. Use this chutney as a side with cutlets, tikka, barbecued veggies, or as a dressing.

Preparation time: 5 minutes
Cooking time: 5 minutes
Total time: 10 minutes
Servings: 4

Nutritional Values:
- *Calories 8*
- *Total Fat 0.1 g*
- *Saturated Fat 0 g*
- *Cholesterol 0 mg*
- *Sodium 152 mg*
- *Total Carbs 1.7 g*
- *Fiber 0.4 g*
- *Sugar 0.7 g*
- *Protein 0.4 g*
- *Potassium 59 mg*

CHAPTER 8 «DRINKS»

Winter Refresher

Ingredients:

- 1 lemon
- 1 orange
- 1 tbsp fresh ginger
- 5 cardamom pods
- ¼ tsp peppercorn
- 1 cinnamon stick
- 6 cups water

How to prepare:

1. Cut orange and lemon into slices and smash the cardamom pods. Peel the ginger and slice it up.
2. Add all ingredients to a pot and bring to a boil. Once boiling, stir and reduce the heat to a simmer. Let it simmer until the fruit slices break down.
3. Strain the liquid into a glass and serve with sugar if desired.

Preparation time: 5 minutes

Cooking time: 20 minutes

Total time: 25 minutes

Servings: 12

Nutritional Values:
- *Calories 17*
- *Total Fat 0.2 g*
- *Saturated Fat 0 g*
- *Cholesterol 0 mg*
- *Sodium 4 mg*
- *Total Carbs 4.3 g*
- *Fiber 1.3 g*
- *Sugar 1.6 g*
- *Protein 0.5 g*
- *Potassium 68 mg*

Banana Green Smoothie

Ingredients:

- 1 cup coconut water
- ¾ cup plant-based milk
- ¼ tsp vanilla extract
- 1 heaping cup loosely packed spinach
- 2-3 cups frozen bananas, sliced

How to prepare:

1. Blend everything until smooth and serve.

Preparation time: 5 minutes
Cooking time: 0 minutes

Total time: 5 minutes

Servings: 1

Nutritional Values:

- *Calories 308*
- *Total Fat 4.9 g*
- *Saturated Fat 1 g*
- *Cholesterol 0 mg*
- *Sodium 352 mg*
- *Total Carbs 61 g*
- *Fiber 8.9 g*
- *Sugar 36.6 g*
- *Protein 10.2 g*
- *Potassium 1,643 mg*

Cinnamon Coffee Shake

Ingredients:

- 1 cup cooled coffee (regular or decaf)

- ¼ cup almond or non-dairy milk

- A few pinches cinnamon

- 2 tbsp hemp seeds

- Splash vanilla extract

- 1.5 frozen bananas, sliced into coins

- Handful of ice

How to prepare:

1. Chill some coffee in a sealed container for a couple of hours (or overnight) before making this smoothie, or be ready to use more ice.

2. Add the non-dairy milk, cinnamon, vanilla, and hemp seeds to a blender and blend until smooth. Add the coffee and cut bananas and keep blending until smooth.
3. Add the ice and keep blending on high until there are no lumps remaining. Taste for sweetness and add your preferred plant-based sugar or sugar alternative.
4. Transfer to a glass and serve.

Preparation time: 5 minutes
Cooking time: 0 minutes
Total time: 5 minutes
Servings: 2

Nutritional Values:

- *Calories 73*
- *Total Fat 2.2 g*
- *Saturated Fat 0.3 g*
- *Cholesterol 1 mg*
- *Sodium 9 mg*
- *Total Carbs 11.7 g*
- *Fiber 1.6 g*
- *Sugar 6.2 g*
- *Protein2.3 g*
- *Potassium 235 mg*

Orange Smoothie

Ingredients:

- 1 cup orange slices
- 1 cup mango chunks
- 1 cup strawberries, chopped
- 1 cup coconut water
- Pinch freshly grated ginger
- 1-2 cups crushed ice

How to prepare:

1. Place everything in a blender, blend, and serve.

Preparation time: 5 minutes

Cooking time: 0 minutes

Total time: 5 minutes

Servings: 2

Nutritional Values:

- *Calories 155*
- *Total Fat 0.6 g*
- *Saturated Fat 0.2 g*
- *Cholesterol 0 mg*
- *Sodium 130 mg*
- *Total Carbs 36.6 g*
- *Fiber 6.9 g*
- *Sugar 29.1 g*
- *Protein 2.9 g*
- *Potassium 576 mg*

Hot Chocolate

Ingredients:

- 3¼ cups almond milk
- 2/3 cups semi-sweet chocolate chips
- 1½ tsp ground cinnamon
- 1/8 tsp chili powder
- 1 tsp vanilla extract
- pinch of cayenne pepper

How to prepare:

1. Add all ingredients to a saucepan and heat until chocolate melts.
2. Serve and enjoy.

Preparation time: 5 minutes

Cooking time: 5 minutes

Total time: 10 minutes

Servings: 2 cups

Nutritional Values:

- *Calories 931*
- *Total Fat 94.3 g*
- *Saturated Fat 82.8 g*
- *Cholesterol 0 mg*
- *Sodium 77 mg*
- *Total Carbs 26.4 g*
- *Fiber 9.7 g*
- *Sugar 15.3 g*
- *Protein 9.2 g*
- *Potassium 1,046 mg*

Raspberry Mojito

Ingredients:

- ¾ cup sugar
- ¾ cup water
- 1 package raspberries
- 1 sprig fresh mint
- 3 tbsp lime juice, freshly squeezed
- 6-8 oz sparkling mineral water
- Crushed ice

How to prepare:

1. To make the basic syrup, add the sugar, water, and raspberries to a saucepan over medium heat. Mix

occasionally until it starts to stew. Lower the heat and delicately stew it for 5 to 7 minutes.

2. Allow cooling then strain the syrup.
3. Muddle 3 to 4 tbsp of the syrup with 1 sprig of fresh mint at the bottom of the glass.
4. Add the lime juice, sparkling mineral water, and some crushed ice to the glass and stir.

Preparation time: 15 minutes
Cooking time: 10 minutes
Total time: 25 minutes
Servings: 4

Nutritional Values:

- *Calories 145*
- *Total Fat 0 g*
- *Saturated Fat 0 g*
- *Cholesterol 0 mg*
- *Sodium 2 mg*
- *Total Carbs 38.7 g*
- *Fiber 0.3 g*
- *Sugar 37.7 g*
- *Protein 0.1 g*
- *Potassium 27 mg*

Berry-Lime Smoothie

Ingredients:
- 1 cup blackberries
- 1 cup blueberries
- 1 tbsp lemon rind
- 2 cups purple grape juice
- 10 ice cubes

How to prepare:
1. Blend all ingredients in a blender and serve.

Preparation time: 5 minutes
Cooking time: 0 minutes

Total time: 5 minutes

Servings: 1

Nutritional Values:

- *Calories 336*
- *Total Fat 1.7 g*
- *Saturated Fat 0.1 g*
- *Cholesterol 0 mg*
- *Sodium 8 mg*
- *Total Carbs 80.3 g*
- *Fiber 12 g*
- *Sugar 65.6 g*
- *Protein 5.8 g*
- *Potassium 1,119 mg*

Cucumber Watermelon Limewater

Ingredients:

- 5 large lemons, halved
- ¼ small watermelon, sliced
- ½ cucumber, peeled and sliced
- ¾ cups sugar
- 8 cups water

How to prepare:

1. Juice the lemons and pour the juice into a pitcher. Add the 8 cups of water, sugar, watermelon, and cucumber and stir thoroughly.

2. Serve as desired. For a boost in flavor, let it chill in the refrigerator overnight.

Preparation time: 15 minutes
Cooking time: 0 minutes
Total time: 15 minutes
Servings: 8 cups

Nutritional Values:

- *Calories 85*
- *Total Fat 0.1 g*
- *Saturated Fat 0 g*
- *Cholesterol 0 mg*
- *Sodium 8 mg*
- *Total Carbs 23.2 g*
- *Fiber 1.1 g*
- *Sugar 20.3 g*
- *Protein 0.6 g*
- *Potassium 85 mg*

Pumpkin Smoothie

Ingredients:

- 1 cup unsweetened non-dairy milk
- 2 medium bananas, peeled and cut into quarters and frozen
- 2 medjool dates, pitted
- 1 cup pumpkin puree (canned or fresh)
- 2 cups ice cubes
- ¼ tsp cinnamon
- 2 tbsp ground flaxseeds
- 1 tsp pumpkin spice

How to prepare:

1. Blend all ingredients in a blender and serve.

Preparation time: 5 minutes
Cooking time: 0 minutes
Total time: 5 minutes
Servings: 2

Nutritional Values:

- *Calories 372*
- *Total Fat 5.3 g*
- *Saturated Fat 0.9 g*
- *Cholesterol 0 mg*
- *Sodium 69 mg*
- *Total Carbs 77.7 g*
- *Fiber 12.8 g*
- *Sugar 48.6 g*
- *Protein 9.5 g*
- *Potassium 891 mg*

Turmeric Smoothie

Ingredients:

- 2 cups non-dairy milk such as almond, soy or coconut
- 2 medium frozen bananas broken into pieces
- 1 cup frozen mango or other fruit
- 1 tsp ground turmeric peeled and grated
- 1 tsp fresh ginger, peeled and grated
- 1 tbsp hemp seeds flax or chia seeds
- ¼ tsp vanilla extract, non-alcoholic preferred
- ¼ tsp ground cinnamon
- 1 pinch ground pepper

How to prepare:

1. Blend all ingredients in a blender and serve

Preparation time: 5 minutes

Cooking time: 0 minutes

Total time: 5 minutes

Servings: 2

Nutritional Values:

- *Calories 264*
- *Total Fat 4.4 g*
- *Saturated Fat 0.8 g*
- *Cholesterol 0 mg*
- *Sodium 128 mg*
- *Total Carbs 51 g*
- *Fiber 5.9 g*
- *Sugar 33.9 g*
- *Protein 9.2 g*
- *Potassium 604 mg*

SHOPPING LIST FOR A PLANT-BASED DIET

- Bananas
- Berries (all kinds)
- Cocoa powder
- Salted almond butter
- Unsweetened vanilla almond milk
- Hemp seeds
- Kale
- Pomegranate juice
- Filtered water
- Cottage cheese
- Vanilla protein powder
- Maple syrup
- Vanilla extract
- Flaxseed Meal
- Coconut oil
- Agave
- Fresh mint leaves
- Spinach
- Rolled oats
- Dates
- Almond extract

- Salt
- Chickpea flour
- Onion powder
- Garlic powder
- White pepper
- Black pepper
- Nutritional yeast
- Baking soda
- Green onions
- Brown rice syrup
- Pears
- Cinnamon
- Basic Polenta
- Apples
- Lemon juice
- Walnuts
- Onions
- Carrot
- Celery
- Paprika
- Curry powder
- Dried thyme
- Dried red lentils
- Apple cider vinegar

- Dijon mustard
- Vegan vegetable stock
- Tomato paste
- Bay leaves
- Butternut squash
- Raw cashews
- Fresh rosemary
- Allspice
- Mustard seeds
- Cumin seeds
- Oregano
- Potatoes
- Celery
- Brown green lentils
- Red Miso
- Blackstrap molasses
- White beans
- Quinoa
- Tahini
- Avocado
- Gluten-free pasta
- Fresh basil
- Pine nuts
- Vegan parmesan cheese

- Lettuce
- Olives (all kinds)
- Dried Dill
- White or red wine vinegar
- Extra virgin olive oil
- Lemons
- Almonds
- Probiotic powder
- Zucchini
- Brussels Sprouts
- Vegan butter
- Arrowroot starch
- Ground turmeric
- Fire roasted tomatoes
- Oil-packed sundried tomatoes
- Flour
- Onion powder
- Cashew cream
- Honey
- Fish sauce
- Rice noodles
- Frozen shelled edamame
- Bell peppers
- Fresh cilantro

- Soy sauce
- Sesame oil
- Coconut milk
- Sriracha
- Reduced-sodium tamari
- Doles flakes
- Super-firm tofu
- Vegan sausages
- Sake or mirin
- Cabbage
- Ramen noodles
- Scallions
- Togarashi seasoning
- Hot sauce
- Haka noodles
- French beans
- Mini sweet peppers
- Broccoli heads
- Teriyaki sauce
- Corn starch
- Brown rice
- Red cabbage
- Cayenne powder
- Jasmine rice

- Barbecue sauce
- Coconut oil
- Pineapple
- Red pepper flakes
- Tempeh
- Grape seed oil
- Chipotle powder
- Toasted coconut
- Dairy-free dark chocolate
- Oranges
- Aleppo pepper flakes
- Dark chocolate chips
- Coconut cream
- Peanut butter
- Granulated sugar
- Graham cracker crumbs
- Vanilla coconut yogurt
- Chia seeds
- Ketchup
- Salsa
- Cucumber
- Liquid smoke
- Capsicum
- Coriander seeds

- Caraway seeds
- Cardamom pods
- Peppercorns
- Grape juice
- Watermelon
- Pumpkin
- Ground flaxseeds

CONCLUSION

The primary focus of the plant-based whole-food diet plan is to minimize your consumption of processed foods as much as possible and replace them with more plant-based and whole natural foods proven to be beneficial in not only improving your health but also stimulating effective weight loss. Hopefully, the information in this cookbook helped clear away confusion and doubts regarding this kind of diet plan.

The whole-food plant-based diet plan is more flexible and understanding than other diets, too. It is mostly comprised of plant-based foods, but you can also have some animal-based products. The extent of animal-based foods in your diet plan depends on your personal choice to entirely not eat them or to consume them in moderation. In general, the more of your meals that are plant-based, the more beneficial the diet will be for you.

CPSIA information can be obtained
at www.ICGtesting.com
Printed in the USA
LVHW082351200819
628393LV00028B/676/P